What others say about the authors

Mark and Cathryn Warburton, of Acacia Law, are incredibly well-informed and passionate about protecting their client's interests. They draw from personal as well as professional experience in this field which means they give powerful advice from the mind, as well as from the heart.

Lindsay Spencer-Matthews
Author, Mentor, Psychologist, Speaker
www.greatchangemaker.com.au

Mark Warburton is The IP Guru. He is a power-house when it comes to intellectual property protection and litigation. He has a wealth of technical knowledge, a quick mind and a determination to secure and enforce patents and other IP for his clients.

Michael Crowley
Business Coach

A proactive and solution orientated IP specialist – my first impressions of Cathryn Warburton. Recent IP issues in our business have gone unresolved with consultation from IP specialists, however, in just a few minutes explaining my issues, Cathryn has provided a range of avenues available to provide much-needed resolution to these challenges.

Paul Crake
Director, Total Ability
www.totalability.com.au

Cathryn is without doubt your go-to coach for anything related to intellectual property. In addition, she has a laser-focused intellect, combined with a genuine concern about her clients - a winning combination.

Carolyn Smith
CEO, My Career Groove
www.mycareergroove.com

I had the pleasure to work with Cathryn Warburton; she is very knowledgeable, caring and looks after her clients very diligently. I would totally recommend Cathryn's business.

Francesca Moi, "The Meetup Queen",
Director, Empowering Events
www.empoweringevents.com.au

Bulletproof

Your

Brand

By Cathryn Warburton

Publication Information

First published July 2018

Published by MJL Publications July 2018 with permission from Cathryn Warburton

MJL Publications
17 Spencer Avenue
Deception Bay QLD 4508
Australia

www.mjlpublications.com.au

LEGAL LIONESS is a trade mark of Cathryn Warburton and Mark Warburton.

Author photos by Melly S photography.

The author would love to hear from you!
Send any comments, questions, compliments or concerns to:

lioness@acacialaw.com
or
cathryn@mjlpublications.com.au

ISBN# 9780994327857

Dedication

This book is dedicated to our two children, who are our true treasures.

Also dedicated to Valerie Nel, a constant and reassuring presence and support in our lives.

Contents

Foreword

Your brand identifies who you are and what you stand for so your ideal audience can connect and engage with you on an emotional level, creating meaning behind your marketing.

Your clients gain a feeling of your personality, values, purpose and motivations so they can know, like and trust you before they buy from you.

It becomes part of your essence, the foundation you build a business on and a compass to keep you pointing in the right direction.

That's why it is so vital to ensure no one can take it from you and why this book is so important for all brands, no matter how large or small.

Cathryn knows first-hand what it's like to lose the things you care deeply about and was inspired at a very young age to become the lioness who looks out for others. Her legal insight and down-to-earth explanation of trademarking and brand protection are vital so you know what to do BEFORE you have no choice but to walk away from the brand you have developed, nurtured and grown.

You have worked hard to create a brand, so right now is the best time to ensure your brand remains yours. You deserve to be well known, well paid & wanted.

Lauren Clemett
International Award Winner, Best-Selling Author, Founder Ultimate Business Propellor

1. Introduction from the Legal Lioness

Hello! Congratulations on taking the first step to Bulletproofing Your Brand, by picking up this book.

The only way to protect your brand is to register it as a trade mark in your countries of interest.

This book is designed for you to pick through it in any order you like. Feel free to read about the topics you are most interested in first.

Browse through the info-graphics and see what takes your fancy or what topic speaks to you.

Flick to the last chapter for a quick cheat-sheet of trademark essential information.

This book is jam-packed with practical tips and information accumulated over 40+ years of combined intellectual property law practice; including both authors personally arguing before three judges in a court of appeal in a trademark case. Which we won, despite being the underdogs.

If you want to know more, we have free and paid online courses at:

www.acacialaw.com
www.legallioness.com

2. Trademark Trouble Is Bound to Find You

Trademark trouble is bound to find you at some stage if you don't have your name registered as a trademark.

Having a company or business name or domain name will not save you from trade mark trouble.

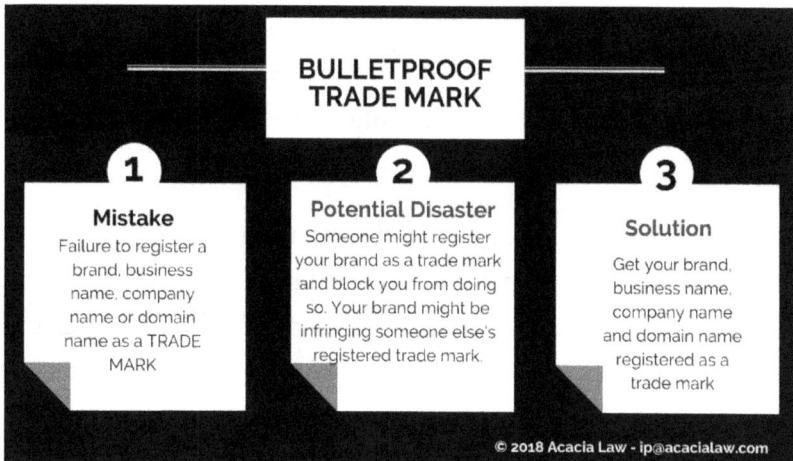

Just this week I saw a client, who is a business coach, an amazing lady, giving so much of herself to the community. She had previously registered her business name, her domain name, and her company name. Now she wanted to get her trademark sorted out. She wanted a trademark registration.

Before seeing me she had not realized that a trademark registration is the strongest type of protection, and it overpowers any of those other kinds of registrations.

She thought she was safe because she had her business name registered. She was wrong.

So I did a search for her, and it was so frustrating! Somebody else had the exact same name already registered as a trademark. So that means, that for the past 18 months, she has been infringing somebody else's registered trademark. Not only that. It was registered before she even started her business. So she could have known about the prior brand if she had taken the right steps to start with.

Now, she's facing having to potentially pay all of her profits to the registered trademark owner. That is so gut wrenching. Everything she's done for 18 months and her profits might belong to somebody else. Plus, of course, she's got the drama of having to rebrand, when she's identified with that name for so long, it is so frustrating, not to mention costly.

I wonder, do you have your business name registered as a trademark? Because if you don't, the longer you delay, the more likely you are to have trademark trouble impacting your business at some stage, because generally, the first to file a trademark has the stronger rights.

3.   Intellectual Property Basics

- Intellectual property (IP) is not physical property, like land or equipment. It is, for example, the right to monopolise:
    - a name (trade mark)
    - an invention (patent)
    - a design (registered design)
    - copying or modifying (copyright)

Main Types of Intellectual Property:

Trade Mark - protects brand name & logo	Patents - protect the way something works
Intellectual Property	
Registered designs - protect the way something looks	Copyright - protects against copying of text, images etc.

- Some common issues arise for each type of intellectual property. These include:
    o Ownership
    o Protection (which may include registration)
    o Enforcement
    o Commercialisation
    o Avoiding inadvertently infringing other's rights
- Obtaining the correct intellectual property protection can save tens of thousands of dollars.
- Getting the right advice early on can help you to set up your intellectual property to best effect and avoid costly mistakes that are difficult to fix.
- Registered intellectual property rights can add substantially to the value of your business.

4. Is it worth the effort of registering a trade mark?

In my view, it is not only worth the effort, it is an essential risk minimising strategy for all small businesses to have their business names registered as trademarks.

A trademark registration is the only defence to a trademark infringement allegation (check to see if this is the legal position in your country; it is the legal position in Australia and New Zealand and many other countries).

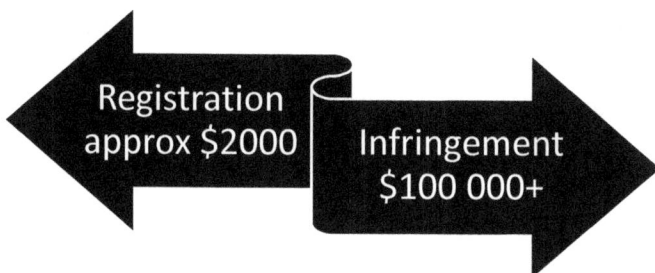

Registration approx $2000

Infringement $100 000+

A client of mine once offered a stranger online a job. The stranger repaid my client's kindness by adopting my client's business name and registering it as a trade mark. To add insult to injury, the stranger then sent a cease and desist letter to my client demanding that she stop using his registered trade mark.

Well the stranger was right. My client was technically infringing his registered trade mark.

My client was understandably furious at the trademark infringement allegation and she wanted me to tell the stranger to jump in the lake.

Unfortunately, the legal position is that the first to register a trade mark generally has stronger rights. I explained to my client that we could get the stranger's trademark removed from the trademark register, but in order to do so we would need to go through the courts, which would cost at least $100,000.

In the end, my client opted to spend $35,000 on rebranding and legal fees to make sure that she didn't get sued for trade mark infringement. Before adopting her new brand name, she made sure that it was registered as a trademark. She is now secure in the knowledge that she has a complete defence to any future allegations of trademark infringement.

5.   Brand Monetizing Process

The process to monetize your brand is really a simple 3-step process.

1.   Create or select a brand,
2.   Protect that brand by registering it as a trademark in your countries of interest,
3.   Build the goodwill and leverage to make money from the trademark.

6. What is a trademark?

The word trademark is used in different ways in industry, marketing, the legal profession and the media. It is therefore helpful for me to provide you with a definition so that you understand the meaning and context in which I am using the term "trademark".

a. What Is A Trade Mark?

A trade mark is a "sign" that acts as a "badge of origin" and differentiates your business, product or service from those of competitors. Think of how live-stock are branded so that you can tell which farm or ranch they come from; trademarks serve a similar function.

b. What Is NOT a Trade Mark?

Having your business name or company name registered, or a domain name registered gives you no trademark rights.

Some business names, company names or domain names might be capable of being registered as a trademark. You only receive trademark protection in those names if they are placed on a Trademark Register (that is, officially registered as a trade mark by the government department in your country of interest).

It is important to be aware of trademark registration scams, which I dealt with later in this book. If you receive an invoice for trade mark registration fees, forward it to your trade mark attorney or a lawyer that you trust. Remember, no government department will send you an invoice for trade mark registration fees unless you have filed a trademark application with them. If you receive an invoice from a country or registry that you have not apply to register with, it is most likely a scam.

If you have received such an invoice, feel free to email it to me, and I will do a check for you at no charge. Send to tmscamcheck@acacialaw.com.

c. **What Different Types Of Trade Marks Are there?**

- Logo (some kind of picture, such as the McDonald's "golden arches" or Acacia Law's tree logo).

- Word/s eg Acacia, Legal Lioness, IBM, Microsoft, McDonald's
- Advertising slogan "Acacia Law – We've Got You Covered"
- 3 dimensional shape eg shape of Toblerone chocolate
- Sound eg Microsoft tune whenever you boot up a Microsoft product
- Smell eg "smell of freshly mowed grass"

7.   10-step Trademark Registration Process

These steps are discussed in the following chapters.

10

STEPS OF TM REGISTRATION

1

SELECT A STRONG TRADE MARK
Avoid rooky mistakes in trademark selection.
Make sure you select a strong trademark.

2

GOOGLE SEARCH
If the name is already used descriptively in your
industry, it is likely to be too descriptive to register

3

TRADE MARK REGISTER SEARCH
Has someone already registered that TM? Check
your local online trademark register.

4

DECIDE HOW TO PROTECT YOUR TRADEMARK
You have the option of:
1. done for you option
2. assisted trademark filing online course
3. seat of your pants (DIY)

5

DONE FOR YOU OPTION
Select an experienced and qualified trade mark
attorney to take the process off your hands.

6 ## ASSISTED FILING OPTION
See more information at www.legallioness.com or

7 ## TRADEMARK IS FILED AND EXAMINED
The intellectual property office will examine the trade mark for problems. A notice may issue if there are official concerns about the application.

8 ## ACCEPTANCE
Once objections are overcome the application may be accepted. Depending on what country the application is in, an acceptance fee may be payable.

9 ## OPPOSITION
Most countries have an opposition period during which others can lodge a formal objection to your trade marks. Oppositions are relatively rare.

10 ## REGISTRATION CERTIFICATE
If no opposition is filed (or if you win the opposition) then a registration certificate will issue.

8.   Selecting a strong trademark

SELECTING A STRONG TM

1 A trade mark must distinguish your business from your rivals

2 It must not already be registered (or used) by someone in Australia in your industry

3 Names not usually used in your industry are best. Think of "Apple" for computers

4 A business name, company name or domain name gives you no IP rights, only a TM rego does

AVOID WEAK & DIFFICULT TO REGISTER TMS

1

Avoid surnames or forenames eg. Jones or Joe, (but a combination of first name and surname often can be registered).

2

Avoid terms that are common or descriptive in your industry. For example, "soft" for fabric softner.

3

Avoid Geographic names, such as street names, suburb names, city names, state or county names, country names etc. For example, Brisbane or Glee Rd or Queensland or Australia.

"a strong trade mark is essential"

a. Descriptive vs Distinctive

To be registered as a trade mark your mark must be "distinctive" and not descriptive of your goods/services. For example, you could not register the word "soap" as a trade mark for soap (because other soap manufacturers would want to use the word soap when describing their soap products).

A good example of a distinctive trade mark that is non-descriptive, is Apple for computers. The word Apple is not at all descriptive of computers, so other traders who want to use the word Apple would only do so to trade off Apple Inc's reputation. Of course, if you own a fruit company or a fruit juice company, the word "Apple" would be descriptive and not registerable as a trade mark as others in that industry would need to use that word to describe their goods.

In my decades in the intellectual property business, I have had many clients come to me after having their logos and branding designed by a marketing company. Unfortunately, some marketing companies focus only on the marketing aspect of branding, and seek to create branding which is descriptive of the client's goods or services.

Purely descriptive branding cannot be registered as a trademark. This means that it is very difficult to prevent others from trading off any reputation that the business might build up in such a trademark or branding.

To be registerable a trademark must be "distinctive" of your particular goods or services. Non-distinctive names or phrases (which are likely to be impossible to register as trademarks), are ones which tend to:

• describe your goods or services (eg "gloss" describes the finish of a photograph, or type of paint)

• be words or phrases that others in your industry might legitimately want to use (eg "best cafe in town" or "food delicious")

• say something good or descriptive about your goods or services ("we only serve vegetarian food" or "gluten-free")

• say something about the type, quality or quantity of your goods or services (eg 200ml describes the size of a fruit juice)

• some surnames are difficult, if not impossible to register as trademarks. The more prevalent they are in Australia or New Zealand, the less likely you are to be able to get them registered.

• real names or stage names or signatures can be registered, provided a letter of consent is supplied by the person of that name. Things become complicated where a famous person has registered their name as a trademark, and somebody else wishes to use their own name quite innocently in the same industry. If you trade under your own name, we recommend that you register it as a trademark.

• Geographic or place names can also be problematic, unless they are unrelated to the goods. For example, "Arctic" might be registrable as a trademark for bananas, but Queensland would not be. This is because bananas are produced in Queensland and others might want to use that name in relation to their bananas, as an indication of where the bananas were produced. On the other hand, "Arctic" is what is called "fanciful" in relation to bananas, as no one producing bananas would need to use that name because bananas not produced in the Arctic.

HOT TIP: have your trademark concepts considered for distinctiveness by your trademark lawyer before these concepts are developed by a marketing company or graphic designer. It is best to know if your ideas are too descriptive of your goods or services to be considered registrable trademarks, prior to spending money on developing marketing materials.

The more distinctive your brand name is in relation to your goods or services, the easier it is to obtain trade mark registration protection for it.

The less the trademark relates to your industry, the easier it will be to register.

Having said all of that, if you have a name which has some descriptive elements, you can sometimes get it registered if you are able to prove that it has actually become distinctive of your goods or services. This can be done by filing evidence of distinctiveness through use. This can be a somewhat complex process and has limited success.

Another alternative is to have a distinctive logo designed, and file a trademark for the words plus the logo may be registerable as a trademark in some countries. We do not generally advise that logos and words be registered together, because this limits the breadth of protection of the trademark to the combination of the logo and words.

However, in cases where the words on their own are descriptive, we do sometimes suggest that a combination of logo and words are filed as a trademark.

It is important that the logo should be distinctive. You should own copyright in the logo. You can do this by having it designed for you (make sure you get something in writing to say that you do own the copyright in the logo to avoid any doubt about ownership and to over-rule any standard terms that the designer might have conferring copyright ownership on them).

Please note that if you use an image under license, you will not be permitted to register it as a trademark, even if the license entitles you to use it in a commercial manner. If you do manage to get it registered, it will be vulnerable to removal on the basis that you do not own the copyright in the logo.

Also, make sure that the logo is not one which is common in your industry. For example, logos of houses would be common in the real estate industry. Your logo would need to be something that sets it apart from others in the same industry, to be considered to be distinctive.

HOT TIP: Avoid selecting a descriptive trademark. Descriptive brands are very difficult, if not impossible to register as a trademark. This means that competitors would be able to use the same or even identical brand to the one you adopted, even if you have built up an extensive reputation in your brand or (unregisterable) trademark or business name or company name.

Distinctive trade marks (eg "Apple" for computers) are the easiest to register as trademarks and the easiest to enforce.

Examples of "descriptive" (unregisterable) brands

AppStore – Reported news.com.au (December 2014). Trademark refused. Apple appealed to the courts, appeal refused. Apple could not register this trademark because they could not show that the term AppStore was one used only by themselves. Most people would agree, and the evidence showed, that the term AppStore is generic and simply describes the store that sells mobile phone applications, which are commonly referred to as "apps". Apple's trademark application for AppStore was also refused in the USA.

STARTUP - Reported news.com.au (December 2014). For some unknown reason, Apple believed that they could monopolise the term "startup" as a trademark in Australia. They were wrong.

9.   Google Search

When I am creating a new brand or trademark for myself, I start with an initial idea, and then I do a Google search for the words.

This search is to see whether:

* the name that I am considering is already a descriptive term in my industry, or
* someone else's already using it as a brand.

a.   Prior descriptive use

If someone is already using those words as a description in my industry or in a similar industry, then I select a different name. Even if your search shows no prior use of a descriptive term, a trademark may be refused for any term that the intellectual property office believes is too descriptive of the goods or services applied for under that particular trademark.

It is difficult, if not impossible, in most countries to obtain registration for a descriptive name, such as, "Australian Lawyers". The reason for this is that Australian lawyers generally would want to use those words to describe their businesses, and it would be unfair to lead one particular firm monopolise that name.

This is different from our brand names, such as, "Acacia" or "Legal Lioness", which are not common descriptions for more firms or lawyers.

When you are considering whether or not an aim is descriptive, you need to consider it in relation to the goods or services that you offer, as well as similar goods or services. Generally, if somebody else in your industry or a similar industry would need those words to describe their business, goods or services, then the name is too descriptive.

There is one exception to this descriptiveness rule. If a distinctive logo is added to the descriptive words, that combination is often allowed to be registered as a trademark. Whether this is allowed and the extent of protection this will give you, will differ from country to country.

Generally, it is best to obtain registration for words on their own, as that gives you a stronger trademark protection. Sometimes that is not possible, and especially if someone has been using a particular brand name for a long time, combining it with a logo can give them at least a chance of obtaining trademark registration incorporating those words (and the logo).

If the name that you are interested in is used anywhere in the world in a descriptive sense, then you may have real difficulty registering it as a trademark. In Australia descriptive words can be registered with the addition of a distinctive logo. Each country has its own rules in this regard.

A trademark registration which is a combination of words and logo, is generally considered to be a weaker form of protection than words on its own.

Cathryn & Mark Warburton: Bulletproof Your Brand

b. Prior application or registration

The situation is more complex if you discover somebody else is already using the name as a brand name or trademark.

This is really something that you would need advice on from a trademark specialist, preferably a registered trade mark attorney. There are simply too many variables to provide helpful general information on this point.

Important considerations will be whether the name is used in your country or only overseas. If it is limited to use overseas, then that may not affect your ability to obtain trademark registration locally.

Is the name used in an industry different to yours? If so, then it may well not be problematic either.

In mid-2014, a small Australian start-up company, managed to generate massive publicity in the media with its claims that Apple Inc. had stolen its name, HealthKit.

The Australian company had the name HealthKit as part of its company name, as well as its business name. It also had the domain name www.healthkit.com registered and the Twitter handle @healthkit. The Australian company complained that Apple should have taken "5 seconds" to do a Google search which would have revealed the existence of its website www.healthkit.com and that Apple would then have realised that the name belongs to the Australian company.

Unfortunately, the Australian company has misunderstood its rights. Ownership of a name is only conferred by trademark registration. Merely having a domain name, Twitter handle, business name or company name does not give the Australian company the rights to stop Apple from using the name HealthKit.

After the story broke and the media, both the Australian company and Apple filed trademarks for HealthKit. It is extremely surprising that Apple did not have its trademark application in place prior to launching its product. (Apple's failure to register iPad in China, before a competitor did, cost it $60 million to buy back the trademark a few years before, so you would have thought that it would have learned its lesson).

Apple and the Australian company will now either need to come to some kind of an agreement about the trademark, or will need to fight it out through the courts to see who is the ultimate victor. Most small Australian companies would not be able to prevail against the limitless resources of Apple, simply because of the costs of defending the rights to register a trademark.

The Australian company could have avoided this disaster, and extensive legal fees, if it had obtained **trade mark** registration for the name HealthKit before it first adopted it. If it had a registered trademark in place, its rights would be much stronger. It would have been able to stop Apple from using HealthKit as a trademark.

If it had a registered trademark behind it, preventing Apple from using the trademark would be fairly simple and cost-effective. Use of an identical trademark on identical goods and services by Apple would be seen to be a blatant trademark infringement, and Apple would likely have been required to pay the Australian company's legal costs. Alternatively, the Australian company would have been in a strong bargaining position to sell their registered trademark to Apple for millions of dollars as happened in China with the trademark iPad.

Cathryn & Mark Warburton: Bulletproof Your Brand

10. Trade Mark search

It is sometimes useful to conduct a trade mark search before adopting a trademark. This will give you an indication of what is already registered as a trademark, and what is likely to be problematic.

Your trademark will only be accepted if it meets all the other requirements, and there is no existing application or registration on the register for goods or services similar to yours.

Trademark searches can be fairly technical and should never be taken as a definitive indication that no problematic trademarks already exist on the trademarks register. This is something that business owners frequently get wrong, and I do not recommend that you should rely on any self-conducted search.

The mere fact that you have not found an identical trademark on the trademarks register does not mean that you can now use that particular trademark. Your search might not have revealed a trademark that is "confusingly similar" to your trademark. For example, if you want to register the name "bandages" as a trademark for business services, and you search for that name and did not find any registrations for bandages for any services relating to business services. Your trademark search could easily have missed similar trademarks that you could infringe by using the name "bandages", and which would prevent you from registering that name, such as:

- Bandage
- B@ndage
- Band@ge
- Bandijiz
- Trandage
- Plasters

When deciding whether or not trademarks can coexist on the trademarks register (or whether the trademark that you are using amounts to an infringement of an existing trademark), the following will be taken into account:

1. whether the trademarks look similar

2. whether the trademarks sound similar

3. whether the trademarks convey similar ideas

The Intellectual Property Office or the court will consider three of these factors and decide whether they believe it is likely that there might be confusion between the respective trademarks.

When these legal tests are applied, some trademarks which seem to be quite similar can sometimes be allowed to coexist, and some trademarks which seem at first glance to be quite different, can be considered to be "confusingly similar" and not allowed to coexist.

TM search Process

NOTE: this is for a very BASIC search and does not guarantee you will find all relevant trade marks. It is only a STARTING POINT in your research.

Database

Find the Trademark database in the country you want trade mark protection in.

STEP 01

WORDS

STEP 02

Type a word or part word into the "part word" field. We suggest you search for each word in your mark separately. Search for misspellings and alternative words with similar meanings and synonyms etc.

Class

Select the relevant class and associated classes. Click the link for more detail on how to select the relevant classes

STEP 03

STEP 04

Status

Select "Pending & Registered" to avoid old and de-registered marks showing

Review Results

Click "search" and review the results. Marks similar to your may prevent you from obtaining registration, and owners could sue you for TM infringement

STEP 05

What does it mean if you want to register a 2-word trade mark and your search reveals one of those words are already registered as a trademark?

This is a tricky question to answer without a concrete example. The only answer that can be given in a vacuum, is that it depends on the circumstances, and the trademarks involved.

Most trademark cases have stated that if your trademark is a word that is contained within an already registered trademark, then your trademark is not registrable, and use of your trademark might infringe the prior trademark. For example, there was a case of VICKS VAPORUB. Someone wanted to register "Vaporub" either on its own, or with another distinctive name. The court held that the prior trademark registration of "VICKS VAPORUB" would stop anybody else from registering the word "vaporub" either on its own or with any other words.

Another example might be, if somebody else has registered "Yellow Horse" for business services, and you wish to register "Horse" for business services, you are unlikely to succeed, as the prior trademark is likely to prevent your trademark registration.

On the other hand, if you have "Horse Business Services" registered as a trademark, and somebody else wishes to register "Rabbit Business Services" they would be likely to succeed, because the overlapping words "Business Services" are common and descriptive in the business industry, and the distinctive part of the trademarks "Horse" and "Rabbit" are quite different from each other.

I had a large biscuit manufacturer as a client. At one stage they brought out a new label for a new range of biscuits. Their usual process was to ask us to do a trade mark search to ensure that their new brands and labels did not infringe any existing trademarks. For some reason, this label had not been sent to us for searching until the day before the biscuits were to be delivered to retail stores. Unfortunately for the client, the brand name they had selected had already been registered by a competitor of theirs in the biscuit industry. The client had spent $90 000 on packaging for that particular brand. We advised them to scrap the packaging and select a new brand name and get us to search the trade marks register first, before they printed new packaging. They had to stop all shipments to retail stores. Their competitor never knew how close they came to infringing their registered trade mark. If our client had put the biscuits on the market with the infringing packaging, they would likely have been sued by the trade mark owner, which would have cost them a lot more money in legal fees and potential damages.

11.   Done for you, assisted or seat of your pants?

The following options are available when seeking trade mark protection.

In the past, the only two options have been to have it done for you by an intelligent property professional, or to give it a go yourself.

HOW DO I REGITER MY TRADE MARK?

1

Done-for-you
Get an experienced trade mark attorney like Cathryn Warburton to secure your trade mark for you

2

Assisted Filing
Do it yourself with an experienced TM attorney showing you how to do it and checking before you file.

3

DIY*
Do it yourself with no support, for those who like to fly by the seat of their pants and figure it out themselves. This option is not recommended

© 2018 Acacia Law - ip@acacialaw.com

We have created third option, which is an "assisted filing" online course. This takes you through the various considerations that we as trademark attorneys work through before filing trademark applications.

Working through such a course can significantly increase the chances of your trademark not only being registered, but also registered for the correct goods and services and classes.

We have seen too many business owners attempted to file the trademark applications themselves, and make mistakes, either by filing for trademarks that a professional could have told them immediately would never have been accepted, or seeking protection in the wrong classes. This is the reason we created the online assisted trade mark filing course.

If you want to know more please email assistedTM@acacialaw.com or go to www.acacialaw.com or www.legallioness.com

12.   Classes and Specifications

The trademark register is divided up into 45 different classes.

These classes are determined at an international level and can be viewed by searching the internet for "WIPO Nice Classification".

Each type of goods or service is slotted into one of those 45 classes. For example, shoes are in class 25, while shoe stores and business services are both in class 35.

You will infringe a registered trademark if you use the same or similar trademark on the goods or services for which it is registered (or similar goods or services).

As an example, "Nike" might be registered in class 25 for footwear, clothing and headgear. They might not have a registration in class 35 relating to retail outlets or online stores. However, if you filed a trademark application for "Nike" in class 35 for such services, you would be refused registration due to the Nike trademark registration in class 25.

Also, if you decided to open up a store selling clothing and footwear, and you decided to call the store "Nike" this would amount to an infringement of the "Nike" trademark for footwear and clothing, even though you are using the name for services that would fall into a different class.

Hot Tip: When drafting your specification of goods and services, do not make it too restrictive. I had a client once who was advised by the intellectual property office to limit his specification to "wooden toys". An infringer adopted and used his trademark on plastic toys. They claimed to be entitled to do this because he had a limited his specification to "wooden toys". If his specification had been properly crafted, he would have had no trouble stopping the infringer.

13. International Trademarks

Trademarks are generally registered in a particular country or region (such as the European Union). This means that if, for example, you file a trademark application in Australia, once it is registered, the protection will extend only to Australia.

It is possible to file an international application, which designates several countries. Before filing the international application, the trade mark must first be filed in a "home" country (eg in Australia) and then can be extended to an international application designating particular countries of interest. The international application will result in the trademark being examined in each individual country in which you have requested protection. This means that it can be objected to in any of the countries for which protection has been requested.

Each country designated in the international application will raise a filing fee (fees differ from country to country). It is also possible to extend the application to the European Union by paying one European fee.

The international application, also known as a Madrid protocol application, can only designate countries which are signatories to the Madrid protocol. A list of the protocol countries continues to grow as more and more countries join the International registration agreement. A full list of countries who have joined the Madrid protocol can be found on the World Intellectual Property Office website at www.wipo.int

14. Common mistakes to avoid

COMMON TRADE MARK FILING MISTAKES TO AVOID

Any of these mistakes can spell disaster for your trade mark protection & waste your money

1. WEAK TM

A weak trade mark can be difficult to register or enforce. See your info-graphic on "Selecting A Strong Trade Mark" to minimise this risk

2. TM FORMAT

Generally a TM should be registered as plain words (and a second one registered for a logo). But if you have a weak mark, we might recommend you register it as a combo word + logo mark

3. TOO NARROW

Government fees are charged per class. So if you have selected, say, class 25, why limit your specification to "socks"? Select the broadest goods you can, eg clothing, headgear, socks and footwear. This gives you broad protection, without any additional cost

4.UNNECESSARY CLASSES

Every class selected increases the costs ($330 government fee per class). Some self-filers select multiple classes that they do not need and waste thousands of dollars

5. ALREADY REGISTERED

If someone else already has the TM you want registered, you could:
1. be stopped from getting your rego,
2. be infringing the prior mark if you use yours (even if you have a business name / co name etc registerd)
*** This could be serious risk and you likely need specific legal advice

6.SCAM ALERT!

Once you file your TM, you will start receiving invoices from scammers who get your details from the TM database. Do NOT pay these. Shred them. Only pay IP Australia online, or invoices that come from Acacia Law. The scams promise you trade mark protection, but they are bogus. If in doubt, email them to cathryn@acacialaw.com to double-check for you (no charge for this)

7.OBJECTION

Official objections are not uncommon. Some can be overcome. Some spell doom for your application. We can assess the objection for a small fee, including providing options, chances of success and potential future costs

8. LOGO

Get written confirmation that you own copyright in your logo, or you won't be entitled to register it as a TM. Cheap designers or template logos can mean you don't own the copyright

15. Copyright trap lurking in your logo

In order to obtain valid trade mark registration, it is necessary to own the copyright in the logo.

If you designed the logo yourself, you will own the copyright automatically.

If someone else designed the logo, you will need to obtain written confirmation from the designer that you own the copyright (if you do not already have such confirmation).

If the logo is one which is taken from a licensed image (even if you paid a licence fee) or clip art or copied from the internet or something similar, then you will not own copyright in the logo. We may still be able to obtain trade mark registration if that is the case, but the copyright owner would be entitled to have it removed at a later date if it became aware of the registration.

If someone else designs a logo for you (even when you provide instructions as to the concept and look that you want to incorporate into the logo), you need to ensure that you own copyright in the logo. The best way to do this is to get your designer to put it in writing that they assign any copyright in the logo to you.

If you do not, you could end up with a logo in which you do not own copyright and which you are not entitled to modify or register as a trade mark especially if their terms and conditions say that they retain ownership.

Sometimes you can obtain trademark registration for such logos, but the registration may be invalidated if it is challenged by the copyright owner, which may be the designer in many instances.

Getting cheap logos designed online can be risky. As an experiment, I requested a cheap logo to be designed for myself via a well-known outsourcing site. When I then searched for that logo on Google images, it turned out that the logo had been directly copied from the logo of a large international company.

If I had registered that logo as my own, they could likely have had my trademark invalidated on the basis that they owned copyright in the logo, and as such I was not legally permitted to protect it by way of trade mark registration.

There may also have been a question of whether I had infringed copyright in the logo.

Copyright Myths

It is a myth that if something is on the internet, you are allowed to copy it.

Another myth is that if a person fails to either state that they own copyright, or fails to imbed a copyright claim into the online image, that it is available for anyone to use.

Avoid copyright infringement

To avoid infringing copyright, simply do not copy the work (including logos) of others. Ensure your designer does not copy either.

If you have a paid licence to use an image, make sure that you have proof of such licence and that whatever you are using it for is permitted by that licence. If in doubt, seek legal advice from an experienced intellectual property lawyer otherwise you could be up for thousands of dollars in copyright infringement damages.

Getty Images and Copyright Infringement

Another example which is becoming increasingly common, is where a web designer or graphic designer designs either a website or marketing material incorporating graphics which they have sourced online; or a graphic designer designs a logo incorporating material sourced online.

The business owner believes that the graphics have been used with the proper permissions, but years later receives a letter of demand from the copyright owner of the graphics (most commonly from Getty Images), and the business owners have no written license agreement to prove that they were entitled to use those graphics.

So-called "free" image websites are dangerous to use, for example, Pixabay, are dangerous. They have within their terms that they do not take responsibility for copyright ownership and if you use an image from their "free" image site, you may have to pay copyright licensing fees to the copyright owner.

Even paid stock image sites can be a source of copyright infringement. I only use images from a site that guarantees they will pay up to $10 000 if I am accused of copyright infringement due to using one of the images I downloaded from their site.

Do not assume that contractors, such as website designers, have copyright licenses for images/text they use on your behalf. Many small businesses assume that images placed on their website by their website designer has the proper license. Make sure you obtain and keep a copy of the license and renew it, if necessary.

To avoid copyright infringement litigation, the business owner must prove that such a license exists, and that the use of such material falls within the terms of the license. On a practical level, this means that all licenses should be kept for material which has been sourced from outside of the business. Alternatively, businesses should create their own material.

NOTE: most licence agreements do not allow you to registser any of their images as a trademark or part of a trademark.

16. Benefits of Registering your Trade Mark

Trade Mark registration has the following benefits:

    a. The trademark protection extend throughout the country in which you have it registered, such as, Australia.

    b. The trademark is valid until a renewal is due, which is generally every 10 years in most countries.

c. Trademark registration protects your brand, unlike other registration such as a company name, business name or domain name registrations.

d. Trademark registration is a complete defence to trademark infringement in some countries, such as Australia.

e. Registered trademarks can be sold or licenced. They therefore are an important business asset. If you're wishing to franchise your business, which is usually impossible unless you have your trademark registered in the countries in which you wish to franchise.

f. Trademark registration confers a brand monopoly, meaning that you can stop competitors from using your brand on your goods or services.

g. A competitor cannot steal your mark and register it as yet their own in the country in which you have it registered.

A trademark <u>registration</u> gives you very strong rights. It can protect your business from having its trademark adopted by a powerful company with deep pockets. If your trademark is unregistered, you are in a very weak position to prevent others from using the same or similar trademark.

A trademark registration is an extremely powerful tool. Imagine your company, however big or small, being able to make sure that the world's 13th richest man could not misuse your trade mark. This is exactly what a small Australian company did recently. The fact that the Australian business had their name registered as a trademark was a major factor in their victory.

Real Life Case – Small Aussie Brow Bar Refused To Be Brow Beaten by French Billionaire

Recently, a small Australian company was table to beat a person described as the 13th richest person in the world (multi-billionaire). The small Australian company registered their trademark "Brow Bar" over a decade ago. The French multi-billionaire's company used the words "Benefit Browbar", for three years in Australia and then filed a trademark application for that name. The Australian company was not happy about this encroachment on their registered trademark. They opposed the French company's trademark application, and were successful based on their prior trademark registration. [Reported in the Courier Mail, 5 April 2015] Given that the local company had "Brow Bar" registered as a trade mark, they could also prevent anyone else from using that name as a brand name.

17. When should you register your trademark?

It is important to consider registering your brand name as a trademark before you start using it.

The first to file a trade mark application generally has stronger rights to the trademark. This means that the sooner you register your brand or business name as a trademark, the better legal position you will be in.

If someone files the trademark application before you they are likely to get it registered. You could possibly have their trademark removed from the register if you used it first, however, costs of such litigation (approximately $100 000 +) is generally well beyond the means of small to medium businesses. Paying approximately $2 000 for trademark protection at the start of the process is a much safer option.

Also, in any trademark dispute, there is no guaranteed outcome, so if you end up in litigation you may lose. That could result in you having to pay legal fees to the registered trademark owner and potentially damages, not to mention the costs of re-branding.

One of my clients told me that she did not want to bother with trade mark protection, if she found out that somebody else had her brand registered, she would simply change her business or brand name and use a different one. I explained to her that she also needed to consider:

a. costs of rebranding,

b. how many sales she would lose by having to change her URL, as her brand name was also her website name,

c. her emotional attachment to the brand (it can be heartbreaking to have two stop using a brand that has become your business identity),

d. the registered trademark owner could sue her for trademark infringement and she would have to either settle by way of agreement or take the matter to court, which could incur considerable legal fees, including having to pay the legal fees of the registered trademark owner, should they be successful in an action against her,

e. potentially having to pay over to the registered trademark owner any profits that she had made under that name as damages.

18.   Shortcut Trademark Selection & Registration Process

You can shortcut the trademark selection and application process by simply buying a business that already has a registered trademark, or by buying a registered trademark from a business (without buying the business itself). This would tend to be more expensive than the process of registration of your own trademark.

> *Real Life Example – Perils of Insufficient Due Diligence - imagine paying millions of dollars for a company only to discover that you had not actually bought the rights to their most important asset, namely their registered trademark "Rolls-Royce"*
>
> The case: Volkswagen's takeover of Rolls-Royce
>
> In an extraordinary oversight, VW failed to seek the rights to the Rolls-Royce brand name as part of its pitch for the company.
>
> This was despite Rolls-Royce directors having made it clear that BMW was their preferred custodian of the Rolls-Royce brand name. RRMC and BMW had already established a joint venture to produce jet engines - with BMW providing the financing and Rolls-Royce the expertise - which was three years away from realising profits.

The situation led to a protracted, expensive and acrimonious legal battle before the European Commission, in which VW questioned RRMC's moral right to control the brand name.

The lesson: do your due diligence

The important lesson from this extraordinary case is that bidding for a company does not automatically give the potential purchaser the rights to produce that company's product.

Had VW conducted an extensive due diligence audit, it would have discovered where the IP rights were held and understood the nuances of associated contracts that allowed production of the key asset: the Rolls-Royce car.

19.   Scam Alert!

Beware of scams offering to advertise your trademark. Typically, these come from overseas and ask for payment of in excess of $1500. The invoice appears to be an official invoice and generally implies (without specifically stating) that this advertisement is necessary for your trademark protection. There is no value to paying this fee. These are scams.

If you have received a payment notification and not sure whether or not it is a scam, feel free to email us on tm@acacialaw.com and we will verify for you whether or not it is a scam, at no charge to you.

Real Life Story – Client Saved $1850 By Doing A Free Scam-Check With Us

One of our clients recently received a request for payment of $1850 to "advertise" his trademark in what looked like an official trademarks journal. The invoice implied that if he did not make the payment, he would lose his trademark rights, or if he did make the payment he would extend his trademark rights.

He sensibly checked with us before making any payment, and saved himself from throwing his money away on a scam.

Example of Scam invoice:

EPTR
EPTR TRADEMARK REGISTER

TRADEMARK 11596095 /1215

EPTR Trademark Register, Morska 35, 75-212 Koszalin

Cathryn Anne Warburton
U13, 59 Brisbane Rd
QLD 4301 REDBANK
AUSTRALIA

Registration number:	
Registration date :	
Application number:	1738193
Application date:	03.12.2015
Class:	16

TRADEMARK REGISTRATION

REPRODUCTION OF MARK:

LAWYER IN YOUR CORNER

Pos.	Description	Curr.	Amount
01	Filing Fee	AUD	2070,00
02	Additional Fee	AUD	0,00
	Total Filing Fee	**AUD**	**2070,00**

PAYMENT:

BY WIRE TRANSFER :
AMOUNT: 2070,00
BENEFICIARY : EPTR
BANK NAME : WBK BANK
IBAN : PL51 1090 1711 0000 0001 1624 7840
BIC/SWIFT : WBKPPLPP
BANK ADRESS : Rynek 9/11, 50-950 Wroclaw, Poland

BY CHECK :
BENEFICIARY : EPTR
ADRESS : UL. MORSKA 35,
75-212 KOSZALIN, POLAND

Please pay the amount, within 8 days by wire transfer or check. Don't forget to quote the trademark number.

Dear Customer,
Please notice, that this form is not an invoice. This is an offer for the annual registration of your Trademark in our Internet database www.eptr-register.com. Please also notice that this offer will become a binding contract with the payment of the amount. The registration on our database has not any connection with an official government organization. There is no obligation for you to pay the amount and we have not any business relation yet. We point on our general terms and conditions on our website. If there are any mistakes or modifications relating to your dates, please inform us to correct or update them.
EPTR Trademark Register sp.z o.o., ul. Morska 35,75-212 Koszalin,Poland VAT PL6692519281 info@eptr-register.com

20. Don't play in traffic, just because your competitors (or the big players) are

Copying what others do does not make you safe

Recently, a client of mine received a letter of demand from Apple Inc. which claimed our client was infringing Apple's :

- Trade marks
- Registered designs, and
- Patents

Our client was horrified. Yes, they were selling the goods in question, but their comment was "we have seen these same products for sale in at least 10 other retail stores for years and Apple has never sued them, so surely we are safe?"

The answer was, "no you are not." The mere fact that someone else might be infringing and has not yet been sued does not mean that you can do the same. Apple Inc. might not have taken any action against those other stores for many reasons including:

- Not being aware of their infringing activity
- They may have licenced those stores to sell those products
- They may have reached a commercial settlement and paid

Apple for the right to sell the
remainder of their stock
- Apple may still be gathering
evidence before launching
proceedings
- Apple may have launched
proceedings and my client might
simply not be aware of it.

That case, which could have cost our client millions, was settled for a few thousand dollars and we managed to negotiate for our clients to become a distributor of Apple's authorised products moving forward.

Real Life Story – Apple's $60 Million Mistake – Failure To Register iPad As A Trade Mark In China (Taken To The Cleaners By A Small Tech Company)

You would think that a large, supposedly intellectual property-savvy business like Apple Inc would be aware that it should register its trademarks throughout the world, before revealing them publicly. Apple has something of a history of trademark bloopers, but failing to register the trademark iPad in China is probably one of its most costly.

A small, almost bankrupt, Chinese technology company hit the jackpot when it had the trademark iPad registered in China. Apple Inc did not give up without a fight, and the case proceeded through the courts. The Chinese company did not give up, and after comments from the judge which indicated Apple that the court's decision would not be a happy one for Apple, Apple reached a settlement agreement with the Chinese company. Apple agreed to pay a massive US$ 60 million to the Chinese company, for the registered trademark iPad in China. This cost, as well as the potential millions spent in legal fees if Apple had paid a few thousand dollars to get their trade mark registered there first.

Media reports state that Apple subsequently has reached iPad sales in China to a value in excess of $8 billion in a three month period, with that amount climbing at the time of reporting.

The sale of the Chinese iPad trademark was a real windfall for the Chinese company, as the situation there was slightly unusual because it was Apple that has created the value of the trademark. Usually, the business selling the trademark builds up the value before sale. Here, the value and the trademark was simply the lack of having registered a trade mark that a multibillion-dollar corporation made famous and, through bad advice or bad planning, failed to secure with a trademark registration in its most profitable market.

Apple Inc had yet another trademark disaster in Mexico.

This could have been avoided if Apple had done its homework.

A Mexican company had registered iFone as a trade mark in Mexico, four years before Apple filed a trademark application for iPhone. In the world of trademarks, if the trademarks sound the same, even if they are spelt differently, the law considers them to be "confusingly similar". For Apple, this means that the prior trademark registration for iFone, would have the same effect as if it was for iPhone. In other words, Apple could not use iPhone in Mexico without infringing the prior iFone registration.

Apple should have conducted worldwide trademark searches and had trademark registrations in place, prior to launching its products. Its failure to have iPhone registered in Mexico resulted in a legal battle.

If the Mexican company had not had a registered trademark in place, it would have been in a very weak position. The fact that it did have a registered trademark in place, meant that Apple could not win. The courts decided that Apple could not use or register its iPhone trade mark in Mexico, as it would cause confusion with the prior registered iFone trademark.

The only options open to Apple at that stage were to:

- purchase the iFone trademark from the Mexican company, or
- sell its iPhones in Mexico under a different name, or
- not sell iPhones (under any name) in Mexico, or
- pay a licence fee to the Mexican owner of the iFone trademark registration

As you can see, the fact of having a trademark registered put the Mexican company in a very strong position. Apple did try to have the Mexican company's trademark removed, but was not successful.

21. When Can You Use the ® or TM Symbols On My Trademarks?

You can watch our cute cartoon 2-minute cartoon video on this topic on YouTube at https://www.youtube.com/watch?v=pG2BhbWyYQU

The TM means 'trademark'. Anyone can use TM in conjunction with their brand or trademark. For example, the brand name 'Acacia Law' can be used with TM in any country, whether or not the name Acacia Law is registered as a trademark in that particular country.

You can use the TM in relation to a registered or unregistered trademark. Using TM does not give you any legal rights, but it does serve the useful purpose of putting people on notice that you are using the name or logo as a trademark.

The ®, or registered trademark symbol, can only be used in relation to a trademark, which is registered as a trademark. Registration as a business name, company name, domain name or any other registration docs not entitle you to use the ® symbol.

For example, if you have the trademark BOOMERANG registered for books in Australia, you could use the trademark BOOMERANG with the registered trademark symbol ® on books in Australia. But you cannot use the registered trademark symbol ® with the word BOOMERANG on books in any other country, unless you also have 'boomerang' registered as a trade mark in that other country.

So, if you wanted to export your BOOMERANG books to New Zealand, you would need to make sure that the registered trademark symbol ® was removed from the any books or advertising material, or first register the brand name BOOMERANG in New Zealand before using that symbol.

You do not have to use the ™ or ® symbols with your trademarks.

It is a criminal offence in most countries to use the ® registered trademark symbol, in respect of goods or services for which the trademark is not actually registered in that particular country.

However, it must be noted that such laws are seldom enforced.

You can use your trademarks without these symbols. If your trademark is registered, you can choose to use either of these symbols, but not both.

If your trademark is not registered, you can only use the ™ symbol. If you are in doubt as to whether your brand or trademark is registered in Australia or New

Zealand, why not e-mail the friendly folks at Acacia Law on TM@AcaciaLaw.com and we will look it up for you?

22. Domain Names

A domain name is a URL or website address. Domain names usually fall into two categories, either:

- descriptive of the business that owns the domain name, or
- consisting of a trade mark/trading name/company name/business name belonging to the business.

Some businesses opt for both types of domain names.

> **HOT TIP:** *Avoid checking to see if a domain name is available, and then coming back to register it later. This can result in your first choice of domain name being registered by someone else, who tries to sell it back to you for an exorbitant price. (This happened to my brother). In some instances, you may be able to prove that the domain name should not have been registered in the name of the other party, but this can be expensive and time-consuming with no guarantee of success.*

The domain name forms part of the intellectual property owned by your business. If you sell your business at a later stage, the inclusion of a useful domain name can increase the sale value.

It is advisable to conduct a trade mark search before using the domain name. If someone else has the same or similar name registered as a trade mark, for goods or services similar to those that you intend to trade in using that domain name, then your use of the domain name would likely amount to trade mark infringement.

Trade mark registration gives much stronger rights and overrides company or business names (even if that company or business name was registered first). For example, if you have registered and use the domain name www.flyinghorsepress.com to publish or sell books, and somebody else has already registered "Flying Horse" as a trade mark for publication services or for books, then your use of the domain name will amount to trade mark infringement in the country in which the Flying Horse trade mark is registered (assuming your services are aimed at or intended for recipients in that country).

A website and its associated domain name can be accessed from almost any country in the world (unlike trade marks which are limited to the country/jurisdiction you register it in).

Business owners sometimes worry whether their domain name might infringe a trade mark which is registered in some obscure country. Certainly, if your website is targeted at people in that country, then there is a chance of trade mark infringement in that country.

However, if your main market is Australia and/or New Zealand, and you have ensured that the domain name is not registered as a trade mark by someone else in these countries (the best way of doing this is to register main part of the domain name e.g. "Flying Horse" as a trade mark), then your use of the domain name will generally not infringe a trade mark.

HOT TIP: Remember to register your trade mark as a domain name early in your planning process. Depending on the business, if you cannot secure the domain name, you might want to choose a different trade mark. It is best to know if the domain name is unavailable, as early as possible in your planning process.

If someone registers a trade mark which is identical to your domain name, but after the date that you registered your domain name, you will be technically infringing their registered trade mark (if you are in the same or similar industry).

The only way to prevent this problem is to register the name as a trade mark yourself. If you do not register the name as a trade mark before someone else does, you may have to enter into a legal battle for the right to continue using your domain name, and that could be very costly.

When registering domain names, it is not necessary to try and register every top-level domain

(TLD) that there is. Eg. acacialaw.com, acacialaw.co.nz, acacialaw.com.au, acacialaw.biz, acacialaw.net, acacialaw.xxx, acacialaw.tv ... the list is virtually endless.

With the introduction of new top-level domains, there are now thousands of domain name suffixes (the part after the first "dot" in your domain name), and more are continuously being added.

I recommend that you register the main ones of interest to you.

There is an entity known as the Trade Mark Clearinghouse. It is possible to provide this entity with details of your trademarks. The benefit of this is that validated trademarks will get priority registration for domain names that become available in new TLDs.

Also, trade mark owners are notified if their names are registered as a domain name in any of the new TLDs (this excludes pre-existing domain name registrations, and pre-existing TLDs such as .co.nz, .com.au, .com, .biz), giving them the opportunity to object to such registrations if they wish.

Cathryn & Mark Warburton: Bulletproof Your Brand

Cybersquatting

Most people will be aware that this sometimes happens with domain names. Businesses sometimes register a whole lot of domain names, with a view to simply blocking the availability of those names to their competitors.

Domain name blocking or cybersquatting is the practice of registering a whole lot of trade marks as domain names with a view to stopping the trade mark owner from being able to use the trade mark. The purpose behind this is to sell the domain name back to the trade mark owner for an extortionist amount.

Cases involving trade marks such as QANTAS and XEROX established that this was illegal and the cybersquatters had to deregister their domain names and pay legal costs to the trade mark owners.

However, it is permissible to register a domain name incorporating a trade mark you have an interest in even if someone else has the same name registered as a trade mark. For example, Toyota is a registered trade mark for hotels and for cars. If the hotel registered www.toyota.com.au they could not be stopped by the car manufacturer.

Cybersquatting is not prohibited in descriptive names. For example, I could not stop someone getting www.intellectualpropertyligitgor.com.au just because I am an intellectual property litigator. Descriptive names are open for anyone to register as domain names.

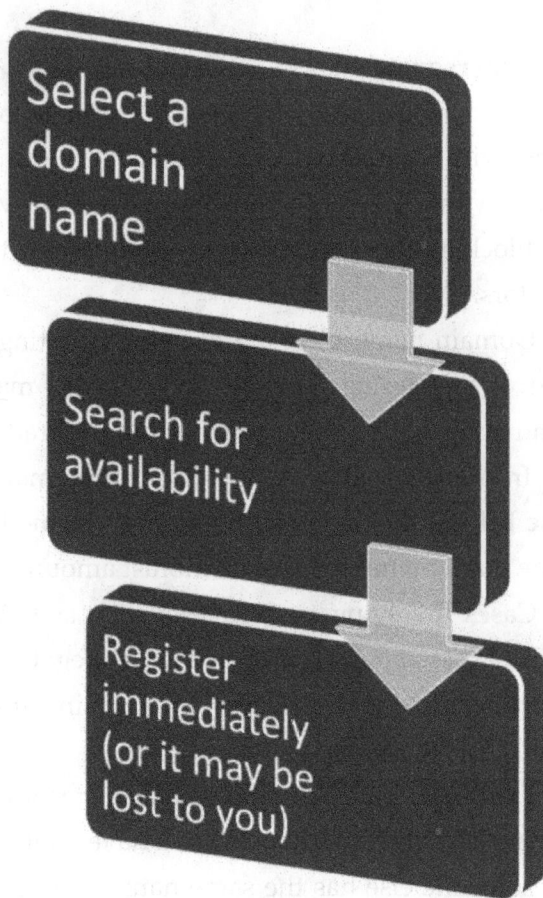

Select a domain name

Search for availability

Register immediately (or it may be lost to you)

23.   Help! Someone is infringing my trademark

First, make sure:

- that you have the trademark registered,
- in the country you allege it is being infringed in,
- that the registration is in your name (or the name of a business that you are authorised to act on behalf of),
- that the registration is valid (for example, has not lapsed due to non-payment of official renewal fees or for any other reason),
- that the goods or services covered by your registered trademark are legally similar to those on which the alleged infringing mark is used.

I recommend that you seek legal advice before sending a letter of demand. This is because in many countries, if you send a cease and desist letter alleging trademark infringement, and certain legal criteria (such as those mentioned above) have not been met, then you could be sued (by the alleged infringer) for "unjustified threats of trade mark infringement".

HOT TIP: Take action as soon as you become aware of someone infringing your trademark or copyright. Delays in taking action can lead to a court later deciding that the intellectual property owner has waived their rights in the intellectual property. This means that they might not be able to enforce it at a later date, even if there is infringement by a different infringer. Often, all that is needed is a letter of demand from a lawyer, especially if you have a registered trademark.

24. Use It Or Lose It!

Once you have a trademark registered, it is important to make sure that you use it. Almost every country in the world has provisions to enable someone to remove a trademark registration if it has not been used for a certain period of time. In Australia and New Zealand, if a trademark has not been commercially used in the three years prior to a trademark non-use removal application being filed, the trademark can be removed from the trademarks register.

If you have your trademark registered for a broad range of goods, and have only used it on some of the goods, it could be removed in respect of the goods on which you have not made actual use of the trademark.

On the other hand, if you have a competitor who has registered a trade mark for a broad range of goods or services, and they are not actually using it on those goods or services, you could have the trademark removed for those goods and services for which the trademark is not being used. The non-use must be for at least three years prior to the non-use removal application.

In years gone by, it was quite tricky to have a trademark removed for non-use, because the person applying to have the trademark removed would have to prove that the registered trademark owner had not used the trademark. Over the years, it became clear that proving a negative (failure to use the trademark) was quite difficult. Some trademarks that had not been used remained on the register simply because the businesses alleging non-use, were not able to prove that the trademarks had not been used.

The law in both Australia and New Zealand changed to make removal of a used trademarks easier. In both countries, the business that believes the trademark has not been used, needs to file the necessary paperwork at the relevant government department. The paperwork only has to allege or say or claim that the trademark has not been used (the person making the allegation does not have to prove the non-use under new laws). The paperwork is forwarded to the registered owner of the trademark.

The owner of the trademark then has to prove that it has made use of its trademark in a commercial sense. So, for example, having letterheads printed but never using them, would be insufficient to show that a trademark had been used for the purposes of defeating a non-use removal application.

This system makes much more sense and is much fairer, because the business using the trademark will be in possession of documentation showing its use of the trademark.

Trademark owners are sometimes approached to consent to registration of a new, similar, trademark. This happens where someone else files a trademark application but struggles to get it registered because your prior trademark application or registration is too similar to theirs. Because your trademark was filed first (provided your application or registration is still valid) your trademark will be blocking the way for theirs to be registered.

HOT TIP: not all types of trademark use would be sufficient to overcome a trademark non-use application. The use must be "genuine commercial use". Over the decades, the courts have set out very clear principles as to what this means. In one case, the sale of over 1 million cigarettes was not considered to be "genuine commercial use" in the particular circumstances of that case.

The owner of the new trademark application might then approach you to consent to having their trademark also placed on the trademarks register. This request for consent to register is usually accompanied by a threat that if you do not agree to having their trade mark registered, then there will file an application to have your trademark removed on the basis of non-use.

If you are confident that you have in fact used your trademark in a commercial sense in the three years prior to receiving that letter, and are able to prove such use, then there is no benefit to you in consenting to the other trademark being placed on the register.

Indeed, if the new trademark application is so similar to your existing trademark, then there is a potential for the public to be confused between the two trademarks. If you find yourself in this situation, I strongly advise that you obtain legal advice from a lawyer well experienced in trademark law.

> *HOT TIP: make sure that you keep make sure that you keep details of your use of your trademark. Documentary proof of your use of your trademark, such as copies of invoices, examples of advertising, copies of newspaper articles etc can be vital in overcoming a non-use removal application, should someone apply to have your trade at some future date.*

Please note that not all lawyers are experienced in trademark law. There is a section at the end of this book dealing with how to select an appropriate intellectual property expert. I recommend that you follow the steps in that guide to ensure that you receive the best possible advice.

It goes without saying that if you have used your trademark, but cannot prove such use, then your trademark might be vulnerable to removal simply because you cannot prove that you have used it.

Some clients are surprised to hear about the non-use removal provisions, and wonder why they exist. The rationale behind these provisions is to ensure that people do not registered trademarks simply to block their competitors from using those trademarks.

Trademark law does not allow trademarks to be used to locked off merely for the purpose of preventing competitors from using them.

The reason why the law gives three years within which to use the trademark is an acknowledgement that with proper business planning, a trademark may be registered a few years before it is intended to be used.

If you file a trademark and, for whatever reason, find that you are not able to make use of it within three years, it might be worth filing a new trademark application for the identical trademark (so you would end up having two identical trademarks), because your first trademark would be vulnerable to removal, but the second one with give you a further three years within which to get the brand used to the extent that it would not be vulnerable to removal.

25.   Help! I have received a cease and desist letter

The easiest way to avoid trade mark infringement is to ensure that you do not start using a trade mark belonging to someone else.

Owning a registered trade mark is a complete defense to trade mark infringement allegations.

If you do receive a letter of demand:

- Do not panic (a hasty response often gets you into worse hot water).
- Do not provide what you consider to be a "helpful" response. Anything you say can (and likely will) be used against you later in the dispute.
- Get advice from a lawyer or attorney who has specific experience in trade mark disputes as they are best placed to help. See the chapter in this book on how to choose your patent attorney or intellectual property lawyer for some tips to select the best person for the job.

Cathryn & Mark Warburton: Bulletproof Your Brand

26. Trademark Checklist

	Select a name – is it one that will give you a strong trade mark (or is it one that others in your industry would want to use – assuming they are not copying you)?
	Prioritise timing of trade mark protection – first to file generally gets the trade mark
	Trade mark search (make sure you are not infringing an existing trade mark)
	Done directly (note: just because the identical mark is not on the Register, does not mean the trade mark is available), or
	Done through Acacia Law. ip@acacialaw.com
	File a trade mark application. If filing via Acacia Law, they include a search automatically. ip@acacialaw.com
	Make sure you complete your trade mark application. Your trade mark application will not be completed if you do not pay all fees. Different countries have different fee policies. There may be more than one payment.
	Do not panic if official objections issue. These can often be overcome.

	Create logo? (Ensure you obtain copyright in logo)
	Register logo as trade mark? (avoid registering logo + brand name as a trade mark unless absolutely necessary, due to limitations in protection)
	File Business Name
	Register domain names
	If overseas protection is required, file within 6 months of the original application (to claim the filing date of the original application)

27. Quick Trademark "cheat-sheet"

When should you file?	The first file a trade mark usually has stronger rights. If a competitor files your business name or brand name as a trade mark before you do, you could lose your rights, and end up infringing their trade mark. This could incur tens of thousands of dollars in legal fees, as well as having to pay over your profits to them. For this reason, filing for trade mark protection as soon as possible, is highly recommended.
What if I already have a company name registered?	A trade mark registration is different from a business name or company name registration. Only a registered trade mark gives you the right to stop others from using the same or similar mark.
Main benefits of trademark registration	The main benefits of trade mark registration are: a. Others are prohibited from using your trade mark (or one confusingly similar to yours), for the goods or services that you have it registered for (or for similar goods / services), and

	b. It is a complete defence to trade mark infringement allegations, for your registered goods and services.
Trademark classes	The trademarks register is divided into 45 classes. How many classes you need will depend on the nature of your goods or services to be protected under the trade mark. Each additional class attracts additional government fees. Obtaining protection in additional classes means that your trade mark is protected for a wider variety of goods or services. Within each class you need to specify exactly which goods or services you want your trademark protected for. In some countries you can select a broad range.
Geographic limitation	Trademark protection would be for the country in which you register it only.
Duration	A trademark last for a fixed period of time, before it needs to be renewed and a government renewal fee paid. The initial and subsequent duration of a trademark is most commonly 10 years, but may differ from country to country.

Removal for non-use	If you do not make commercial use of your trade mark for a fixed period (often 3 or more years), it can generally be removed from the register, and you will lose rights to it. A minority of countries require you to actively prove you have made commercial use of your trademark in that country. For these reasons, we recommend keeping records of how the trade mark is used, including examples of the use, for example, photographs of labels, signage, business cards, websites, invoices etc showing the trade mark in use (these must be dated).
Extending protection overseas	Most local trademark applications can be extended overseas within 6 months of the local filing, to secure overseas protection and obtain the benefit of the local filing date. As the first to file generally has stronger rights, this gives you the advantage of the earlier filing dates. This only applies to participating countries (most countries participate in this scheme). Alternatively you can file for a new application directly in an overseas country of your choice (provided you meet their local requirements).

How long does it take to secure trademark registration?	It can take between 7 ½ months and several years for the relevant government department to issue a trademark certificate, from the date of filing. The sooner you file for trade mark protection, the better for the commercial confidence of knowing that the brand you have selected can actually be protected by way of trademark registration.

Brand Story – From Coward to Legal Lioness

When tragedy struck, I was just six years old. My three year old friend disappeared. As the search for Mishak dwindled, I could not understand why everyone was not still out looking for him. Nor could I understand why they called it a search "party", when it was an unimaginable nightmare.

The sound of Mishack's mother wailing like a wounded animal, the smell of the dry African dirt, the confusion and the terror of it all remain with me to this day. So many times in the days, weeks and even decades that followed, I wondered if anybody could have done anything to have prevented the tragedy.

More importantly, I wondered if there was anything I could have done, or should have done, that might have made him more aware of stranger danger.

Where was he? Was he cold? Was he lonely? Surely he must be scared? Did he think no one was looking for him? What was he eating?

The questions were endless. And there were no answers. As days turned into weeks, then months, then years, still no answers came. Only questions echoing in my mind.

That nightmare shaped me into the protector that I would later become.

I chose a legal career, because I felt it was a way that I could not only honour my lost friend, but also make a real difference to those who needed help.

Unfortunately, Mishack was never found, although a core group of family and friends continued to search for him year after year.

Eventually even the police had to admit that he was likely dead. They said that there had been a spate of young boys kidnapped in the area and their best theory was that they were murdered and their body parts used for black medicine rituals (a detail that still makes me ill to this day, and certainly one that I should never have overheard as a small child imagining what had befallen her friend).

After the nightmare of my friend disappearing, I became hypervigilant, watching out for danger on behalf of others. It made sense for me to go into a career where I would be trained to help others avoid potential disaster.

Of course, I could never have gone into criminal law. What if I ended up in a court room with the person who had abducted my friend, and I didn't even know it? No way, that was too much of a risk for me. Instead, I went into another branch of the law.

I help people protect their businesses and intellectual property. Working in this field means that I am protecting their families' livelihood, and therefore protecting the existence they have built for their families, which is very satisfying to me.

I find it particularly fulfilling when I can help people before they get into legal trouble. This is why I put so much effort and time into creating free online videos to help business owners keep out of legal hot water. Friend me on Facebook to get access to these videos - https://www.facebook.com/LegalLioness.

I am now known as the "The Legal Lioness". I am the recipient of multiple international business awards.

I have a passion for protecting businesses from business bullies (having been bullied mercilessly myself as a child, this is another "hot-button" issue for me), and bringing business communities together. I would love you to share about your business on my business Facebook group https://www.facebook.com/groups/BizBoosters/

Drawing First Blood At 13

It was a sheep's heart, literally dripping with blood, that fostered the spirit of the Legal Lioness in me when I was just 13.

As I think back, I am once again on that hot school bus. The stuffy air hardly circulating, even though all the windows were open (no air-conditioning for kids back then). As usual, I was feeling sick to my stomach. The bus ride home was torture. He was there. The Bully, with his posse always egging him on to new levels of verbal and physical cruelty.

I was a coward and I knew it. I would do anything I could to avoid confrontation. I would suffer humiliation if I thought it would help me escape quicker. I had sleepless nights, and nightmares. Flashbacks and former humiliations frequently ran through my mind, even when he was nowhere in sight and a chance encounter was unlikely.

Little did I know that that was the day I would learn that you do not have to be physically strong to overcome impossible odds. All you need is courage, determination and knowledge.

If you can't be strong, you must be clever. That was the day, The Legal Lioness was born in blood.

That day, I also learned, that being strong for others is my strength.

I have no idea why I decided to stand up to The Bully on that particular day. Half of me was screaming in my head that I was totally mad and I was going to be pulverised, but I had had more than I could stand. As the

Bully stepped towards me to do his worst, I reached into the plastic bag at my feet. He did not even notice me do it. He was watching my face. Looking for fear in my eyes.

The sheep's hearts we had dissected in biology that day, which the teacher had kindly given me as a treat for my cat, were cool in my hand and slippery, dripping with blood.

Suddenly, I was totally calm. No matter what the cost, today I was not going to just take whatever indignation this brute decided to hand out.

He stepped closer, checking back over his shoulder to make sure his gang was watching. I remember his unconcerned, but puzzled face as I stood up … this was a change from my usual cowering between the seats.

Then, no one could believe it. I couldn't believe it! I stepped towards him.

He faltered slightly, but quickly stepped forward to meet me. Smirking. He was huge, like the Hulk I had seen on TV. A mountain of flesh. More a man than a boy.

I looked up into that smirk, held eye contact, and pulled the front of his shirt towards me, leaving a gap between the shirt and his chest. Quickly with the other hand I slipped the bloody, raw sheep's heart down the front of his shirt.

And then I saw it. Terror in his eyes. The Bully was afraid of me! Afraid of whatever I had done. He had no idea what I had shoved inside the front of his shirt, but the sensation of raw meat and blood on his chest turned his face whiter than his crisp school shirt.

Then, it was as though he did not see me at all. He brushed past me to the very front seat of the bus. As he got there he ripped the sheep's heart from under his shirt and hurled it out of the window. Trembling, he crumpled onto the seat, hunched and alone.

There was a stunned silence as the other kids struggled to process what they had witnessed. They did not realise what I had done. They had not seen the sheep's heart. All they knew was that, inexplicably, David had slayed Goliath.

In that moment, my life changed forever. I found a power inside me that I never knew existed. The power of the lioness, later to become the Legal Lioness.

I did feel bad for The Bully. I had never intended on total humiliation for him. I was only thinking of self-preservation.

That was the day I learned, if you can't be strong, you must be clever.

The beating I had expected never came. Not that day, nor any other day. The Bully was subdued and never acknowledged my existence again (thank goodness).

When his thugs started messing with the little kids on the bus the next day, he shook his head and said, "They are not worth it."

Just like that, the bullying stopped. Not just for me, but for everyone.

It was as though a curse had been lifted. No one ever discussed it, but I knew, deep inside of me, that I had stood up, not only for myself, but for all of us who had suffered at the hands of the Bully.

As I matured I realised that there were other types of bullies, other types of injustices in the world. I was inspired to become a lawyer, to help those who could not help themselves; those who were taken advantage of, who did not know the secret that every bully has something they fear.

As the Legal Lioness, I now stand between my clients and what I call "Business Bullies". The unscrupulous people who look to take advantage of hard-working business owners. My weapon of choice is no longer a sheep's heart, but the letter of the law, which I wield with power and confidence enough to make the business bullies back off, just like that sheep's heart did with my teenage tormentor all those decades ago.

Always remember, you are unique and you are amazing (even when it does not feel like it). Every small step forward is an improvement on where you were yesterday. You've got this. If I could overcome these (and countless other) challenges, so can you!

Other books

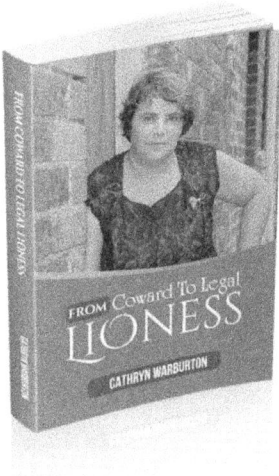

Email : partners@accialaw.com

Business Awards

Acacia law, the firm founded by Cathryn & Mark Warburton received the following awards between 2009 and 2017:

"Stevie Business Woman Of The Year" – October 2017 (bronze medal), Awarded in New York
"Stevie Business Woman Of The Year" – October 2015 (bronze medal), in the professional services category, Awarded in New York

"New Small Business in of the Year" – October 2015 (runner up), Ipswich Chamber of Commerce

"New Small Business in of the Year" – October 2014 (runner up), Ipswich Chamber of Commerce

"Sustainable business of the Year" – Porirua business Excellence awards, November 2010

"Best Professional Services Firm" – Porirua Business Excellence Awards (Runner Up), November 2010

"Most Dynamic IP Firm of the Year – Australia and New Zealand" – Corporate International Global Award – October 2010

"Best IP advisory Firm of the year – New Zealand" – Corporate International Global Award – May 2010

"Wellington Gold Business Awards" – May 2010 (Runner Up)

"Sustainable Business of the Year" – Porirua Business Excellence Awards, November 2009

Speakers Bios

Cathryn Warburton is the Legal Lioness. Determined and courageous, overcoming severe bullying as a child instilled in her a passion to protect others. As a skilled litigator, she indulges in her dream to push-back against business-bullies who target her clients. She is an international award-winning lawyer and patent attorney and 5-time published author. Cathryn bullet-proofs her client's businesses and protects them like a mama lioness protecting her cubs. She makes sure that no business is left without access to affordable, easy-to-understand legal information. She does this through her books, legal workshops and 1-2-1 legal services. She is a popular speaker, having presented to thousands of people.

Mark Warburton is the Intellectual Property Guru. His determination to protect innovation stems from a family legacy in which his grandfather, a genius inventor, had his innovations stolen and patented by someone he trusted, which led to his grandfather dying a pauper on a park bench. Mark is an international award winning lawyer and patent attorney, a registered mediator and 3-time published author. His prowess in the court room sees him winning cases that others thought were unwinnable. Mark's offers pro-bono legal mentoring, proactive legal workshops and 1-2-1 work with clients. Mark is a sought-after presenter, who simplifies complex concepts for his audience.

Legal work, Media, Speaking & Training

Contact : partners@acacialaw.com www.acacialaw.com

Cathryn & Mark are available, together or individually, to assist with the following legal issues, or to give media comment, or for speaking or training engagements on the following topics:

Intellectual property protection, commercialisation & litigation

- Franchising
- Patents
- Designs
- Copyright
- Trade Marks
- Licensing
- Avoiding legal mistakes

Small Business Ownership

- Entrepreneurs
- Legal Essentials
- Spouses working together
- Family work / life balance
- Innovative business strategies
- Running a business while attending to special needs children